THE BEST OF POUCHER'S LAKELAND

BOOKS BY W. A. POUCHER

Overleaf: Climbing Napes Needle

THE BEST OF
POUCHER'S LAKELAND

W.A.POUCHER

CONSTABLE · LONDON

FIRST PUBLISHED IN GREAT BRITAIN 1997 BY CONSTABLE & COMPANY LIMITED
3 THE LANCHESTERS, 162 FULHAM PALACE ROAD, LONDON W6 9ER
COPYRIGHT © 1997 THE ESTATE OF W.A.POUCHER
ISBN 0 09 477060 3
PRINTED IN HONG KONG THROUGH WORLD PRINT LTD

A CIP CATALOGUE RECORD FOR THIS BOOK IS AVAILABLE FROM
THE BRITISH LIBRARY

CONTENTS

My late father was a regular visitor to Lakeland for a period of over fifty years and during this time he amassed a large collection of both black and white negatives and colour transparencies covering the area. Between 1940 and 1963, he produced six books of monochrome photographs of the Lake District mountain scene, the last of which also contained nine pictures in full colour. All these books have long been out of print. His guidebook *The Lakeland Peaks* appeared in 1960 and is now in its tenth edition.

Finally, during the 1980s three books of colour photographs were published (the last posthumously): *The Lake District*, *Lakeland Fells* and *Lakeland Panorama*. As these are now also out of print, the publishers suggested that, from the large collection of colour transparencies of the Lake District passed to me by my father, I select some of the best, not excluding those that had already appeared in print, to form the present volume, the publication of which will enable those lovers of Lakeland's picturesque mountain, valley and lake scenery, to have a permanent record of some of the magnificent views that this beautiful part of our country has to offer.

In consultation with Constable, I have selected one hundred photographs which we consider to be 'The Best of Poucher's Lakeland' and have arranged them in a sequence which starts in the east of the region in Mardale and moves first to the north-west, then through the area of the central and southern fells to end finally in the west at Wasdale. In the Introduction, I give the route followed by this sequence, and have added the approximate location of viewpoints used for them. A map, which also shows this information, appears on pages 12 and 13.

John Poucher
Gate Ghyll,
High Brigham,
Cockermouth,
Cumbria
1997

INTRODUCTION

In case there are any photographers who peruse this book and do not know the terrain, the route that is given below will be of assistance in identifying the approximate location of the viewpoints used for the 100 pictures. It is divided into two sections. The first which starts in Mardale, covers the east and north of the region whilst the second, beginning in Ambleside, runs through the centre, south and west. The accompanying map shows the same, numbered, viewpoints.

First section

The route starts at the foot of Mardale, and runs along the road on the eastern shore of Haweswater (1) on the way to the head of the valley (2,3), from where it goes over Harter Fell (4) and High Street (5) before descending to Patterdale by way of Angle Tarn (6). Once in the valley, it follows the path on the eastern bank of Ullswater (7) to Howtown (8). It now takes the road to Pooley Bridge and along the western shore of the lake (9) as far as Glenridding from where it ascends Helvellyn (10,11). After returning to Glenridding it continues southwards, passing Deepdale (12), Dovedale (13) and visiting Hartsop (14) before reaching the summit of the Kirkstone Pass (15). After descending the other side of the pass as far as Troutbeck there is a diversion to the top to the Garburn Pass (16). On returning to Troutbeck it moves on to Windermere (17).

It now follows the A591 through Low Road (18), Ambleside, Rydal (19) and Grasmere (20), over Dunmail Raise (21) and along Thirlmere (22), after which it forks right through the Vale of St John (23) to join the A66 near Threlkeld. Turning left it follows this road passing beside Bassenthwaite Lake (24). It then returns along the same road as far as the Portinscale junction, which if takes to reach the road which runs above the western shore of Derwentwater (25), then it returns to the A66 and takes the fork to Keswick and Derwentwater (26,27,28,29). It now follows the road to Borrowdale, with a diversion up the narrow Watendlath road as far as Ashness Bridge (30).

After passing through Rosthwaite it turns off to Stonethwaite, where it passes over Rosthwaite Fell (31) to reach the summit of Glaramara (32) and descends over Thornythwaite Fell (33) to the valley and now follows the road to Seathwaite, where it climbs up Sty Head (34) to the tarn. Here it divides, the first direction is up the Corridor Route (35,36) to Great End (37), on to Scafell Pike (38,39) and the Lingmell Col (40). The second direction it takes is along the Climbers' Traverse on Great Gable under the Napes ridges (41,42) as far as the Sphinx Rock (43) and then returns back down Sty Head (44).

Having returned to the valley at Seathwaite, the route runs to the top of Honister Pass, from where it first goes to the summit of Dale Head for the view to the north (45), returns to the top of Honister and climbs Fleetwith Pike (46) before descending the pass on the Buttermere side (47). At Gatesgarth (48,49) it turns up to Haystacks (50,51,52) and returns to Gatesgarth (53) then passes alongside the lake to Buttermere village (54) and continues by Crummock Water (55) to Lanthwaite Green (56) and on to Loweswater Church (57) and Loweswater itself (58). From here it follows the road to Ennerdale Bridge, diverting to Ennerdale Water (59), before taking the fell road to Kinniside Common and its stone circle (60), where this section ends.

Second section

This section begins in Ambleside, where the route takes the road to Skelwith Bridge and Great Langdale passing Elterwater (61) and Chapel Stile (62) before arriving at the New Dungeon Ghyll Hotel. From here it climbs up Stickle Gill (63) to Stickle Tarn (64) and then on to Harrison Stickle (65) and Pike O'Stickle (66) before descending to Mickleden and upRossett Gill (67). It returns to Oxendale (68) and up Crinkle Crags to Long Top (69,70). Then back down to the valley head and along the narrow road (71) to Blea Tarn (72).

It now goes back down Great Langdale to Skelwith Bridge where it takes the Coniston road, but, before reaching Coniston, it branches off to Tarn Hows (73, 74) and from there runs down to Coniston Water and along its east bank (75), round the foot of the lake to Torver (76) and Coniston. Now it ascends Coniston Old Man (77, 78) goes onwards over Ladstones (79) to the summit of Wetherlam (80) from where it goes on to Grey Friar (81) and down to Seathwaite in Dunnerdale (82, 83, 84) and up the valley to Cockley Beck (85).

It now takes the steep and sinuous road over Hardknott Pass and on to Border End (86, 87), back to the top of the pass and up Harter Fell (88), then descends to Brotherilkeld in Eskdale (89), along Upper Eskdale (90) and over Mickledore down to Wasdale Head (91). It now passes through Mosedale up to Black Sail Pass with a diversion to Pillar Rock (92) before passing over Kirkfell (93) and back down to Wasdale Head (94). The route finally runs all the way down the road on the northern shore of Wastwater (95, 96, 97, 98, 99, 100), where it terminates.

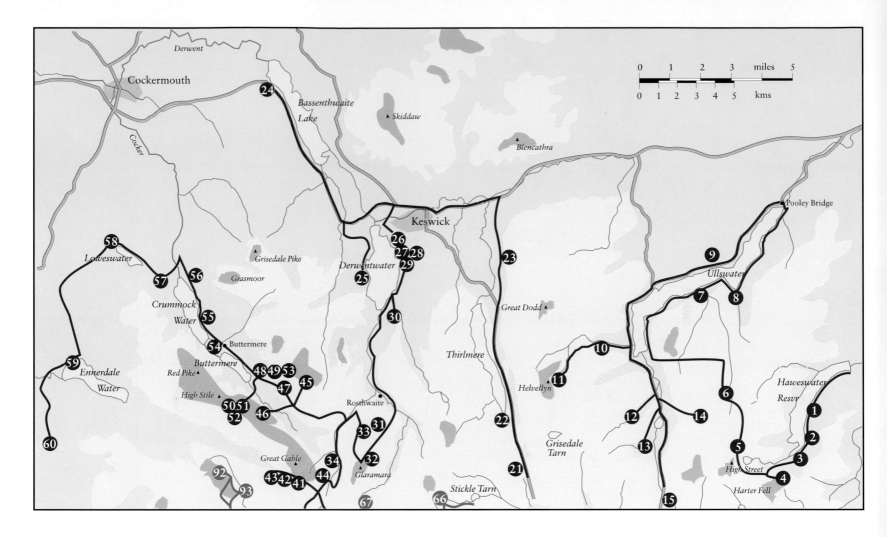

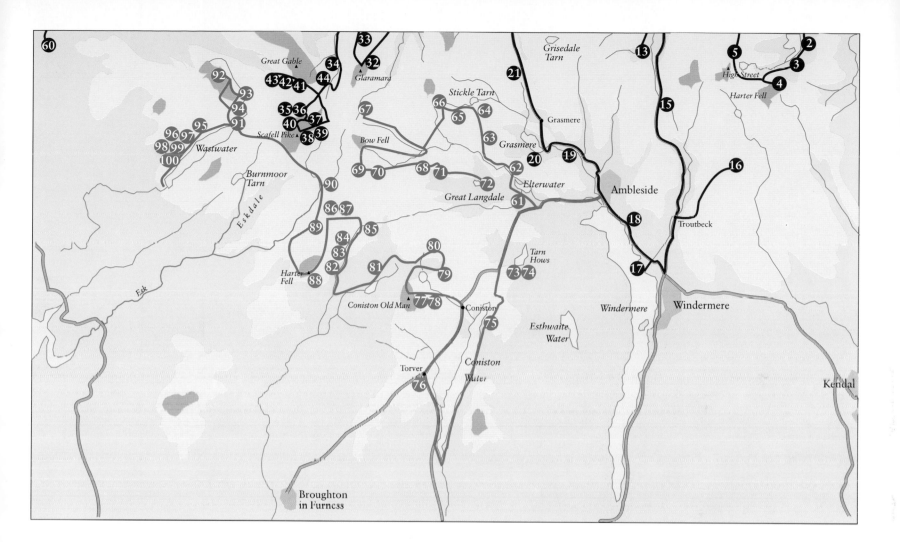

[1]

This lake/reservoir lies on the eastern fringes of the Lake District and is delightfully situated among the hills, offering many opportunities for picture-making. The road leading to the head of the valley runs above the eastern shore and there is a path along the other side. A combination of the two makes a pleasant walk right round the lake.

THE HEAD OF MARDALE

[2]

Fell-walking begins at the end of the road on the left, which may be reached from Glenridding or Penrith. There are several well-trodden paths leading up to all the enclosing hills, none of which presents any difficulty. Examples include the ascent of (*a*) Harter Fell, which dominates the valley head, by way of Small Water and Nan Bield Pass and (*b*) High Street via Mardale Ill Bell or by way of Rough Crag.

THE OLD MARDALE
IS REVEALED

[3]

This dale holds memories for me stretching back nearly fifty years. My diary shows that a friend and I drove to Mardale on 2 January 1937 to drink a last cup of coffee at the Dun Bull Inn. It closed down a few months later, was dismantled and was eventually engulfed by the rising waters of the, then, new Haweswater Reservoir. All that is left of it is the heap of stones in the foreground of this picture: they were revealed in 1973 when a severe drought lowered the water level by some 50 ft and laid bare the remains of the hamlet. Thousands of people again came to Mardale during the droughts of 1984 and 1995, when the ruins were again exposed and the news media carried stories and pictures of the event.

HIGH STREET AND BLEA WATER FROM HARTER FELL

[4]

The spacious view to the west from this peak
reveals a fine prospect of High Street, with
Blea Water, the deepest of the Lakeland mountain
tarns, nestling in the bosom of the green hills
below it.

[5]

A broad and lofty ridge, High Street forms
an immense plateau with a conspicuous stone wall
running north-south along it. A Roman road
once crossed its summit, but traces of this
can be seen only when the westering sun is low.
Long ago High Street was the scene of
an annual fair at which horse-racing was an
important feature and indeed the summit used to
be shown on some maps as 'Racecourse Hill'.
The narrowest part of the ridge is at the Straits
of Riggindale.

HELVELLYN FROM
ANGLE TARN

[6]

This beautiful sheet of water, which is passed
on the descent from High Street to Patterdale,
provides a wonderful foreground for this
picture of the mighty Helvellyn in the distance.
It is also a favourite place for picnics on
a sunny day.

SHEFFIELD PIKE
FROM ULLSWATER

[7]

The middle section of this lake is generally considered its finest, with the beautiful woods of Gowbarrow Park to the north and the slopes of Place Fell to the south. Sheffield Pike is a satellite of Helvellyn.

[8]

The lower section of Ullswater is a popular venue for water-sports which are based upon Howtown, reachable either by road from Pooley Bridge or by way of the delightful path from Patterdale which edges the lake most of the way.

ULLSWATER
AND ST SUNDAY CRAG

[9]

On this calm and serene day, St Sunday Crag –
with its outlier, Birks, to the left – are seen in
the distance from the path on the western shore
of the lake, perfectly mirrored in its still waters.

THE APPROACH TO
HELVELLYN

[10]
The path seen in this picture will be familiar
to all fell-walkers who approach Helvellyn from
the Glenridding side. It rises from Grisedale
along the flank of Birkhouse Moor to reach the
'Hole in the Wall' and then goes on towards
Striding Edge. Nethermost and Dollywagon Pikes
can be seen to the left.

STRIDING EDGE
FROM THE ABYSS

[11]

On this ridge, which affords walkers the most
spectacular ascent of Helvellyn, care is essential
when crossing its narrow rock arête, and
particularly when descending the craggy 'Step' to
the saddle. Thence a rough scramble up the Abyss
leads to Gough's Memorial and the summit cairn.
The views down either side of the Edge are fine –
even sensational. Here, the whole of the Edge is
seen in retrospect: this is the classic picture of it.

[12]

This dale, the first one on the right when driving
to the Kirkstone Pass from Patterdale, does not
present an attractive appearance from the road,
showing only bare grassy slopes. To reach it
you must walk about a mile to Wall End Cottage,
beyond which the slopes to Gavel Pike and
Lord's Seat fall into the dale on the right; for it is
only then that this fine dalehead is suddenly
disclosed. The skyline tops stretch from Hart Crag
on the left to Deepdale Hause on the right;
they form the precipitous eastern façade of
Fairfield and are well worth exploring.

DOVEDALE

[13]
This dale is dominated by Dove Crag, whose Y-shaped gully, a well-known rock climb, is clearly visible from the road. It is separated from Deepdale, to the north, by the undulating grassy ridge of Hartsop above How, which is seen to the right in this picture.

Gray Crag

[14]

The village of Hartsop, seen here with Gray Crag
in the background, lies close to the road which
runs up the northern side of the Kirkstone Pass.
Paths from this village lead to Boardale Hause,
to Hayeswater and eventually to High Street.

[15]

Most visitors to the beautiful National Park will have been over this famous pass, either by car or on foot. Looking northwards down the pass gives a glimpse of Brothers Water, at its foot, with Place Fell beyond.

[16]

The Garburn Pass connects Troutbeck with
Kentmere and is used by many walkers to
reach High Street by way of Ill Bell and Froswick.
From its crest, looking to the north-west, we get
a fine view of Red Screes which dominates the
western side of the upper regions of the
Kirkstone Pass. From near Ambleside a good path
runs up the south ridge of Red Screes to the
summit, from where, people and cars appear in
miniature down on the pass far below.

RED SCREES FROM
THE GARBURN PASS

WINDERMERE

[17]
Windermere is the largest of the lakes. It is more than ten miles in length and its volume equal to that of Ullswater and Wastwater together, and twelve times that of Derwentwater. It is largely devoted to water-sports of all kinds. In this picture, taken from its eastern shore looking northwards, the fisherman on the landing stage, yachts on the lake and the Langdale Pikes in the distance, are very familiar sights to the passing visitor.

THE LANGDALE PIKES
FROM LOW WOOD

[18]

Low Wood, situated on the shore of
Windermere about two miles south of Ambleside,
is an excellent viewpoint for a long-distance shot
of the Langdale Pikes which are seen here to
good effect against a cloud-heavy sky.

[19]

An unusual view of this charming lake – the
photograph was taken from its eastern corner
near Steps End and discloses the true expanse of
the lake, whereas only glimpses of it can be seen
from the road which skirts its northern shore.

[20]
A high viewpoint near Red Bank reveals
this lovely lake in its true setting, enhanced by
the background of hills in which Helm Crag and
Seat Sandal are prominent.

STEEL FELL

[21]
Although only rising to a height of just over
1,800 feet, this fell dominates the view to the west
when approaching Dunmail Raise from the
Grasmere side.

THIRLMERE

[22]
In the valley, where Thirlmere now lies,
there were once two smaller lakes and in the
early 1890s the proposal to link these and
submerge two villages to create a reservoir as a
source of water for Manchester was fought
bitterly by Canon Rawnsley and the Thirlmere
Defence Association, with other eminent men
such as Ruskin in support. However, as so often
happens, the proponents of the reservoir won and
the present Thirlmere was created; but as
seen here, today the scene it presents is still
one of beauty.

BLENCATHRA FROM ST JOHN'S VALE

[23]

A walk through this short but beautiful dale towards Threlkeld is worthwhile, for just off to the left of the road you will find one of the best packhorse bridges in Lakeland. This photograph of it shows Blencathra, with its riven southern face, in the background.

SKIDDAW FROM
BASSENTHWAITE LAKE

[24]

This lake has never achieved distinction because, unlike most of the others, it lacks a fine mountain dalehead. Nevertheless it is a picturesque sheet of water and yields a good view of Skiddaw from its northern end. Its name, however, is notable since it is the only lake actually so named, the others all being either 'meres' or 'waters'.

DERWENTWATER AND BLENCATHRA

[25]

Photographers will find many opportunities to take pictures from the narrow road that runs above the western shore of Derwentwater, as the views across the lake are, in the right conditions, almost breathtaking. Here, Blencathra, with a snowy mantle and some fleecy clouds above, is in the background, with Keswick in the middle distance beyond the lake.

SKIDDAW FROM DERWENTWATER

[26]

This makes a popular subject for holidaying photographers, as Skiddaw is the first mountain seen when they reach the landing stages on the lake. But it is a long hard climb to reach the summit from Keswick, and in my opinion is less rewarding than many of the other fells, although, on a good day, the view to the central fells is worth seeing.

FRIAR'S CRAG

[27]
This popular tree-crowned crag can be used to give 'near interest' to pictures taken from the Derwentwater shore. This view has Causey Pike, left, and Grisedale Pike, right, on the skyline. By moving a little to the right the photographer can include Cat Bells in the encircling ridge.

CAUSEY PIKE
FROM DERWENTWATER

[28]

Causey Pike is more usually photographed from Calfclose Bay or with Friar's Crag in the foreground (see last picture). In my opinion, neither of these viewpoints displays the mountain as effectively as this one, where it is perfectly reflected in the mirror of Derwentwater.

FLOOD

[29]
As Derwentwater is not often flooded like this,
when I observed these unusual conditions,
I thought that a shot of the small cone of Cat Bells
with the ridge leading to High Spy on its left was
a worthwhile subject.

SKIDDAW FROM ASHNESS BRIDGE

[30]

Ashness Bridge carries the narrow road to Watendlath over Barrow Beck and has, over the years, been used as a viewpoint for innumerable photographs. Here, the scene looks particularly attractive with the tapestry of autumn colours leading the eye to the blue of Derwentwater and the noble form of Skiddaw.

TARN AT LEAVES

[31]
This delightfully named tarn, high on
Rosthwaite Fell, mirrors the sky with
Pike o'Stickle, one of the Langdale Pikes,
appearing as a prominent feature in the distance.

LOOKING NORTH FROM GLARAMARA

[32]

Many lovers of Lakeland consider this peak one of the finest in the district because from its summit such an immense panorama is revealed in all directions. This picture looks to the north, where Derwentwater is backed by Skiddaw in the far distance.

GREAT GABLE FROM THORNYTHWAITE FELL

[33]

From the summit of Glaramara a good track
runs down over Thornythwaite Fell to Borrowdale,
and if, on descending it, you glance to your left,
this view of Great Gable and Green Gable will
be revealed. They appear here with a light dusting
of snow on their higher slopes.

ON THE WAY TO STY HEAD

[34]

On the walk up to Sty Head from Seathwaite, the hard work begins after crossing Stockley Bridge. But when you reach the 1,000 ft boulder, the wide rocky valley flattens out, as seen in this picture, and progress becomes easier. One of the most charming sections of the valley has this cascading stream, with the Scafell Pikes looming on the far horizon.

GREAT END FROM THE CORRIDOR ROUTE

[35]
The Corridor Route leaves Sty Head and climbs along the flank of Great End, passing the entrance to Skew Gill which offers a good scramble to the summit for those competent in this sport.

GREAT GABLE
FROM LAMBFOOT DUB

[36]

Great Gable dominates the view all the way
along the Corridor Route. About halfway along it
the ground flattens out and cups the shallow tarn
which is known as Lambfoot Dub. This makes
the best foreground for Great Gable.

SPRINKLING TARN
FROM GREAT END

[37]

The flattish top of Great End is immense, and is
strewn with boulders and cairns. From its
northern edge the finest views are revealed; one
of them is shown in this photograph, taken from
the exit to Central Gully, with Sprinkling Tarn
lying more than a thousand feet below.

[38]

If, on leaving the summit of Great End, you
decide to walk on to Scafell Pike, the highest of
the Lakeland mountains, you will be able to look
across to the cliffs of Scafell, as seen here. They
rise to hem in the south side of Hollow Stones,
and have played an important part in the history
of rock climbing. But as they face the north,
the sun only catches them at dawn, and late on
a summer day.

GREAT GABLE
FROM SCAFELL PIKE

[39]
As you begin your descent from Scafell Pike
towards Esk Hause, glance to your left for
this fine view of Great Gable seen across the
intervening valley, with the more northerly fells
stretching away into the distance.

THE VIEW FROM
LINGMELL COL

[40]

If your preferred route of descent from Scafell Pike
is to Sty Head via the Corridor Route, you will
pass this Col on the way. The flat ground of the
Col opens up superb views of both Lingmell and
Great Gable.

THE VIEW FROM LINGMELL COL

The Napes Ridges

[41]

If, from Sty Head, you follow the 'Climbers' Traverse', you will eventually pass below these ridges which lie on the southern flank of Great Gable. For the enthusiast they offer numerous climbs of varying difficulty. Napes Needle (see next picture) is clearly seen on the right.

CLIMBING NAPES
NEEDLE

[42]

Fell-walkers who wish to inspect – rather than
climb – this famous Needle should ascend the
gully below it and scale the easy rocks on the left
to reach the 'Dress Circle'. Here there is room
to sit at ease and watch any climbers who may be
attempting its ascent. The climb is graded as
HVD (Hard Very Difficult).

WASTWATER FROM THE SPHINX ROCK

[43]

This remarkably shaped rock, likened by some to the profile of a Red Indian Brave, will be found at the end of the 'Climbers' Traverse' on Great Gable, and the stance for this photograph needs a steady head. It is a risky place in which to attempt to change a lens, as there are steep slopes, of about 1,500 feet, below.

BORROWDALE FROM THE STY HEAD TRACK

[44]

The track down from Sty Head Tarn to Stockley Bridge passes the 1,000 ft boulder before the final descent. From here appears this view of Borrowdale in all its glory. It is a very rewarding finish to this long and delightful walk.

EEL CRAGS FROM DALE HEAD

[45]

From the top of Honister Pass it is a relatively
easy walk to the summit of Dale Head from
where splendid views to the north open up.
In this picture Eel Crags, which lie on the
Newlands side of High Spy, are close at hand
with Skiddaw and Blencathra in the far distance.

THE BUTTERMERE VALLEY FROM FLEETWITH PIKE

[46]

A view is not always improved by a lofty vantage point, but in this case Fleetwith Pike yields a superb vista of the valley with Buttermere and Crummock Water nestling between the enclosing fells.

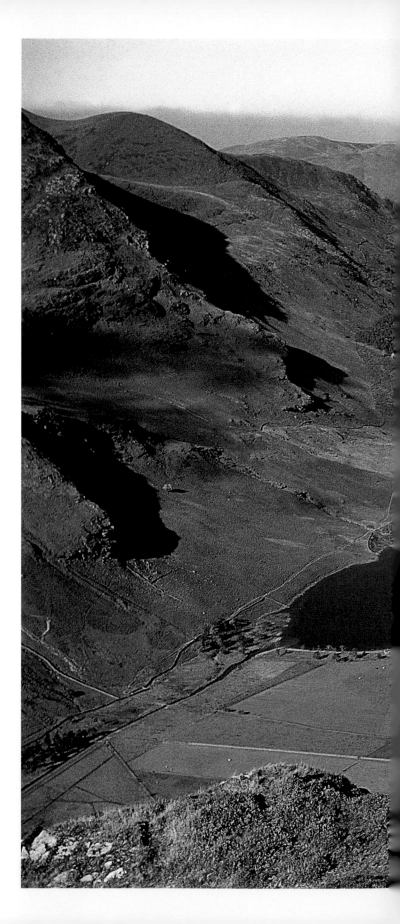

THE HIGH STYLE RANGE FROM HONISTER PASS

[47]

There are only two good viewpoints on the Buttermere side of this famous pass: the first is near the bridge on its summit, but it is the second, near the lower bridge over Gatesgarthdale Beck, which yields this stunning view of the High Stile range. Morning light shows these fells at their best.

HAYSTACKS FROM BUTTERMERE

[48]

I have often been asked which is the most beautiful hill in Lakeland, and have no hesitation in choosing Haystacks, some 1,950 ft high and surrounded by a ring of higher peaks. It is easily reached from the car park on Honister, but a more interesting approach is the walk from Warnscale Bottom. On reaching the plateau, the track, running through heather, passes three lovely tarns by which one may sit and enjoy, in silence, the beauty of one of nature's masterpieces.

REFLECTION

In this striking photograph, taken from almost
the same viewpoint as the last we see, not
Haystacks itself, but only its outline mirrored in
the placid waters of Buttermere.

BLACKBECK TARN

[50]

This is the first tarn encountered on the delightful walk to Haystacks which I mentioned earlier, and this picture catches the sombre aspect which it so often presents. The gleam of sunlight on its surface contrasts well with the Gables silhouetted against a stormy sky.

THE GABLES FROM THE
INNOMINATE TARN

[51]
After a rough scramble from Blackbeck Tarn,
the second lake, the Innominate Tarn suddenly
appears ahead, its surface usually reedy but
reflecting the Gables on a calm day.

[52]

Turning to the right, the path keeps to the shore
of the tarn with Pillar, dominating the scene,
in the background.

HIGH CRAG
FROM BUTTERMERE

[53]

hoever planted the trees round the head
of Buttermere gave a wonderful gift to
photographers, for their inclusion in pictures
of the High Stile range (such as this one of
High Crag) imparts a quality of artistry
missing in other views from this point.

118

FLEETWITH PIKE FROM BUTTERMERE

[54]
A grey day and a still lake reflecting
the mountains always make a good picture.
The only problem is to be there when these
conditions prevail.

CRUMMOCK WATER

[55]

The road on the right twists past the narrows of
this lovely lake and requires special care by
motorists, owing to the frequent passing of
large coaches. In late autumn the colours here
are superb.

HIGH STILE AND RED PIKE FROM LANTHWAITE

[56]

The High Stile range of hills can be photographed from many higher viewpoints to the north, all of which will disclose Buttermere below the peaks. But as I was relaxing on Lanthwaite Green one day, a painter of Lakeland scenes gave it as his opinion that this lower viewpoint yielded the most picturesque view of this group of hills. And so I took this photograph – those who have climbed to the higher belvederes can judge for themselves!

GRASMOOR FROM
LOWESWATER CHURCH

[57]
A beautiful church in such a secluded spot comes
as a surprise, but it makes a good foreground
for Grasmoor, one of the finest belvederes and,
in my early days, least climbed peaks in Lakeland.
The autumn colouring adds to the beauty of the
scene.

[58]

This, the third lake in the Buttermere valley, is seen at its best from its western end, but access to this viewpoint is difficult and the marshy ground very wet underfoot. It opens up a fine prospect of the massive Grasmoor fells.

THE PILLAR RANGE FROM ENNERDALE WATER

[59]

Ennerdale is a very long valley – it seems endless when the rain pours down on the tired fell-walker returning from a long walk in the surrounding hills. The finest scene, unfolded at its western end, is that of Pillar, with just a glimpse (on its left, and behind it) of the famous Pillar Rock. To the right the view encompasses Scoat Fell and Steeple.

THE KINNISIDE STONE
CIRCLE

[60]
If, after visiting Ennerdale, the visitor intends
driving on to Wasdale, the shortest route is by
the fell road from Ennerdale Bridge. This road
at first climbs steeply and then, after passing over
a cattle grid, drops gently down until this
stone circle, one of several in the district,
appears on the left of the road.

THE KINNISIDE STONE CIRCLE

THE LANGDALE PIKES
FROM ELTERWATER

[61]

Visitors on their way to Great Langdale will find
that from Skelwith Bridge, a short walk beside
the River Brathay and thence across some fields
to this pretty little sheet of water, yields an
excellent view of the Pikes.

THE LANGDALE PIKES FROM CHAPEL STILE

[62]

Who has not stopped in surprise and admiration on seeing for the first time the superb profile of this group of hills? The sight of them on a clear day immediately induces the urge to climb them, and they may be ascended from any side without difficulty. The two most popular routes start at the New Dungeon Ghyll Hotel; one goes by Stickle Ghyll and the other by Dungeon Ghyll. Both of them are delightful – my advice is to ascend by one and descend by the other.

THE ASCENT TO
STICKLE TARN

[63]

The paths alongside Stickle Ghyll became so eroded over the years that much restoration work has been necessary. The normal route goes to the left near the prominent waterfalls and eventually emerges on the shore of Stickle Tarn. In this picture Harrison Stickle appears on the left, then a glimpse of Pavey Ark and finally Tarn Crag on the right.

PAVEY ARK
FROM STICKLE TARN

[64]

This magnificent crag dominates the tarn and is
a favourite of the rock climber. Rising diagonally
from right to left is the narrow track known as
Jack's Rake, a sensational and, in places,
exposed route of ascent which should be
severely left alone by all fell-walkers.

A WILD DAY ON HARRISON STICKLE

[65]

I shall always remember the day I took this picture, because as indicated by the immense cloudscape, there was a terrific wind which made it difficult to stand up, let alone keep still, when making the exposure. As the sharpness of this study shows, I eventually succeeded.

GIMMER
FROM PIKE O'STICKLE

[66]

This beautiful mountain scene draws the
admiration of all who stand on the summit of
Pike o'Stickle on a clear morning, with its good
view of Gimmer (a magnet for rock-climbers)
and of Loft Crag above it. Looking down across
the dale below, Blea Tarn is usually clearly to be
seen, and Esthwaite Water is just visible, in very
good weather, on the far horizon.

[67]

Taken from near Rossett Gill, this picture
shows to perfection the characteristic outline of
Pike o'Stickle with its southern flank falling
steeply down to the valley below.

CRINKLE CRAGS

[68]

This rocky ridge separates Great Langdale from Upper Eskdale, and so reveals the hills on either side. There are several easy walks to its summit ridge, which is popular with old and young alike. But the most sporting ascent is by Crinkle Gill, which starts at the footbridge in Oxendale where the Gill is only a short step to the left. This route is suitable for experienced fell-walkers only, and should on no account be followed when the stream is in spate.

THE SCAFELL PIKES
FROM LONG TOP

[69]
Long Top is the highest Crinkle and is an
excellent place from which to appraise the
Lakeland Giants. Together with Bowfell, these
encircle the remote wilds of upper Eskdale.

BOWFELL
FROM LONG TOP

[70]

Long Top rises to the left of Mickle Door
and from here Bowfell is the first peak to catch
the eye, with its many vertical rifts known as
Bowfell Links. It can be reached by walking over
Shelter Crags and dropping down to Three Tarns
before climbing to the summit by the path seen in
this picture.

MICKLEDEN

[71]
This valley, photographed from the road
which rises to Blea Tarn, offers a most
interesting walk for the elderly. It starts at the
Old Dungeon Ghyll Hotel, nestling at the foot
of Pike o'Stickle on the right of the picture,
and leads up the wide green strath to an
old sheepfold at the head of the valley in
the centre. More energetic fell-walkers may wish
to continue along the well-known track to
Esk Hause via Rossett Gill which runs up to the
left from the valley head, passing between
Bowfell and Rossett Pike.

THE LANGDALE PIKES
FROM BLEA TARN

[72]

This beautiful tarn lies beside the narrow
hill-road connecting Great and Little Langdale.
To see it smooth as a mirror means an early visit,
before the wind has ruffled its surface. For this
shot I had to lie down on the tarn's edge,
otherwise there would have been no foreground.

THE PIKES
FROM TARN HOWS

[73]

It is unusual to visit this beauty spot and find no one else there, but this happened to me once on a cold and snowy day in February. During the summer season it is generally crowded, for it undoubtedly merits a visit by any passing traveller. This picture, taken from near the Tarn Hows outflow, shows the Langdale Pikes in the distance.

[74]
Photographing Tarn Hows with the longer
stretch of water in the foreground reveals the
Helvellyn range on the horizon.

[75]

This beautiful lake is best seen by driving
northwards from its southern end on the
twisting road that runs along its eastern shore –
a route which unveils changing views of
Coniston Old Man and its satellites all the way.
Near the end of this drive is Brantwood,
made famous by John Ruskin who declared
that the view from there was the finest in all
the Lakes. It was also a favourite with
Wordsworth who had a seat in the grounds.
Here, across the lake, we see the Old Man with
Dow Crag to its left.

DOW CRAG AND CONISTON OLD MAN FROM TORVER

[76]

From Torver we get closer view of these two fells, both of which are of interest: Dow Crag to the rock-climber and Coniston Old Man to the fell-walker. The Old Man is probably one of the most popular ascents in Lakeland and many visitors, on attaining the summit, try to pick out Blackpool Tower in the vast panorama!

DOW CRAG
FROM THE OLD MAN

[77]

More usually photographed from Goat's Water immediately below, this crag is a favourite with rock-climbers who may prefer this view which reveals its many climbs in detail.

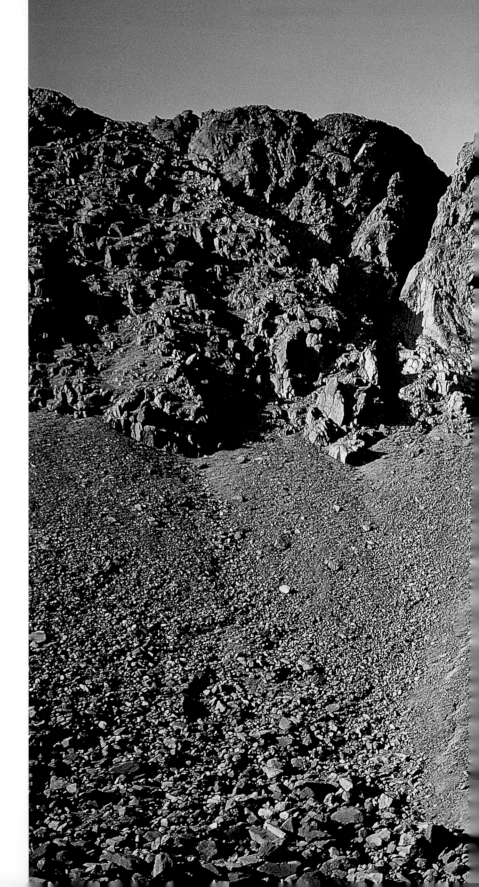

THE SCAFELL PIKES
FROM THE OLD MAN

[78]

Hundreds of walkers attain this popular peak
and after scanning the view to the south, turn
round to admire the Scafell Pikes – a masterpiece
of Nature. From here one can walk along the
broad ridge to Brim Fell and descend to the
Youth Hostel.

LADSTONES

[79]

Walkers who make the long ascent of Wetherlam will notice the remarkable change in its geology when they reach the pile of stones seen in this picture. In the distance is Coniston Water.

PIKE O'STICKLE FROM THE SUMMIT CAIRN ON WETHERLAM

[80]

Wetherlam may be climbed from
several directions, all the routes involving a
longish walk, but the extensive views from
the summit amply reward the effort expended.
I particularly like this aspect of Pike o'Stickle
with its scree gully sweeping gracefully down
to the valley below. Some time ago it was
discovered that Pike o'Stickle was once the site
of an industry – the manufacture of stone-axes
by neolithic man.

THE SCAFELL PIKES
FROM GREY FRIAR

[81]

There are many places on the Coniston Fells
from which you may enjoy the view of these
famous Pikes, but both artists and photographers
have long agreed that Grey Friar is the finest
belvedere of them all.

[82]

Dunnerdale, known also as the Duddon Valley,
although lakeless has a great appeal, and an
autumn drive through it, from Ulpha to
Cockley Beck, can be a real delight, as is
illustrated in this picture.

HARTER FELL
FROM DUNNERDALE

[83]
Because it has no lake this dale is neglected
by many visitors, but as we see in this series of
three pictures, this is their loss. From here,
Harter Fell presents a different aspect to the
more familiar one seen from Eskdale.

HARDKNOTT
FROM DUNNERDALE

[84]

Taken higher up the dale this picture shows the River Duddon in the foreground and Hardknott on the horizon. Over the years the planting of conifers in this valley has increased considerably.

BIRKS BRIDGE

[85]

Situated at Cockley Beck which lies at the head
of Dunnerdale where it joins the road between
Wrynose and Hardknott Passes, Birks Bridge has
great charm. It is a place where fell-walkers often
pause for a break and in hot weather may well
post a lookout and 'skinny-dip' in the Duddon.

ESK PIKE AND BOWFELL FROM BORDER END

[86]

I first discovered this excellent viewpoint as long ago as December 1939, when my son and I spent a fortnight walking over the western fells. I have returned to it every time I have driven over Hardknott Pass, as Border End is only 500 ft above the summit of the pass and, in my opinion, reveals the finest panorama in all Lakeland.

BOWFELL
FROM HARTER FELL

[88]

This mountain is one of the shapeliest peaks
in Lakeland when seen from this viewpoint on
the upper slopes of Harter Fell. It is a favourite
with many fell-walkers and to ascend it from this
side is an arduous task – to climb it from
Langdale is an easier proposition.

THE BEGINNING OF THE WALK TO UPPER ESKDALE

[89]
There are few climbers and fell-walkers who
have not revelled in this walk which passes
many points of interest, including Esk Falls and
the source of the beck in the remote fastness of
the dalehead.

PILLAR FELL
FROM WASDALE

[91]

The whole of the smooth side of this mountain is
seen from Wasdale, where the packhorse bridge
behind the Wasdale Head Inn makes a good
foreground. But the other side of Pillar Fell,
facing Ennerdale, presents a very different picture.

194

THE WEST FACE
OF THE PILLAR ROCK

[92]

Here we see something of the other side of Pillar,
which is not at all smooth. The most interesting
route to Pillar Rock is by way of the 'high level
route' which starts at Robinson's Cairn and
meanders along the mountain side above
Ennerdale. Until you reach it, it is the east face
of the Rock that is visible, but if you continue
the west face comes into view. To photograph the
Rock to perfection you need a sunny afternoon in
summer, for at other times it is dimmed by the
shadow of its parent fell.

THE GABLES
FROM KIRKFELL

[93]

If, after returning along the 'high level route'
to Black Sail Pass, you continue on to Kirkfell
and walk along its summit plateau, with its two
tiny tarns, this view of Great Gable may come as
a surprise, as the mountain has lost all the
splendour of its pyramidal elevation as seen from
Wasdale. From this point its Ennerdale face can
be appraised.

GREAT GABLE
FROM WASDALE

[94]

This is my favourite picture – of a favourite dale and a favourite mountain! The noble pyramidal form of Great Gable is revealed to perfection here, and the bridge in the foreground seems to invite the visitor to cross it and explore the dale – even (if he or she is well shod) to climb the peak for its superb view of Wastwater and the surrounding hills. To me, this picture captures all the glory of the National Park.

THE SCAFELL PIKES
FROM WASTWATER

[95]

These well-known peaks are seen to advantage
from the upper reaches of the lake. From left to
right they are: Lingmell, Scafell Pike and Scafell.
Brown Tongue rises along the valley below them
and is a seemingly endless slog up to Hollow
Stones, seen middle distance, centre – one of
the most impressive places in this group of hills.

[97]

These Screes are unique in Britain, and the millions of stones falling into Wastwater make an impressive picture. As they face north-west they are poorly illuminated until late in the day. The marvellous transformation as the setting sun reaches them, has to be seen to be believed.

[98]
This superb lake is frequently seen by visitors,
but this view of its mirrored surface may come as
a surprise as, due to the prevailing weather, not
only are its waters often ruffled, but sometimes
one can see neither lake not enclosing hills!

HERDING SHEEP
IN WASDALE

[99]
A lucky shot only possible in late autumn, taken
on the lakeside road and showing Yewbarrow,
Great Gable and Lingmell in silhouette against
a threatening sky.

THE GLORY OF
A WASDALE SUNSET

[100]
This photograph catches a marvellous scene
at its best, but I have to confess that it was the
only time that I have ever seen it like this. I feel it
offers a memorable conclusion to this pictorial
tour of the much loved, and so beautiful,
Lake District.